MW00906311

Drotar, David L.

The fire curse and
other true medical
mysteries.

BRI

$15.85

DATE			

The
FIRE CURSE

OTHER TRUE
MEDICAL
MYSTERIES

The FIRE CURSE

And

OTHER TRUE MEDICAL MYSTERIES

David Lee Drotar

WALKER AND COMPANY ☀ NEW YORK

First published in the United States of America in 1994 by
Walker Publishing Company, Inc.

Published simultaneously in Canada by
Thomas Allen & Son Canada,
Limited, Markham, Ontario

Library of Congress Cataloging-in-Publication Data
Drotar, David L.
The fire curse and other true medical mysteries /
David Lee Drotar.
p.   cm.
Includes bibliographical references and index.
ISBN 0-8027-8326-0. —ISBN 0-8027-8327-9 (lib. bdg.)
1. Medicine—Miscellanea—Juvenile literature.   I. Title.
R706.D76 1994
610—dc20   94-5659
                                          CIP
                                          AC

Book design by Ron Monteleone

Printed in the United States of America

2   4   6   8   10   9   7   5   3   1

Contents

Acknowledgments

The author would like to thank the following people for the help they provided during this project:

Lauren Ackerman, Elaine Amabile, Pauline C. Bartel, Beth Bedinotti, Richard Bodman, Jennie Burke, Joanie Caska, Donald Clarke, Pamela Conford, Jackie Craven, Pamela K. Crossley, Stacy Davis, Charlene Douglas, Dorothy Drotar, Karen Drotar, Sheila Flihan, Cara Fortey, Ruth Ginzberg, Dilenia Hernandez, Joyce Hunt, Bojana Jordan, Kate Kunz, Walter Lape, Nadya Lawson,

Peg Lewis, Kristin Lindemann, John MacDonald, Jennifer McGrath, Jerry D. Meranda, Sue Miller, Marie Musgrove, Ann Narciso, Rudy Nelson, Val Nicotina, Vince Nicotina, Patricia Perrone, Nancy Rullo, Sean Sardi, Dianne Schoenberg, Eric Silvester, Jennifer Snell, Jane Streiff, Julia Tobin, Donna Tomb, Frankie Van Meter, Lynn Vanderhoof, and Catherine Wayland.

The
FIRE CURSE

 *And*

OTHER TRUE
MEDICAL
MYSTERIES

Introduction

STRANGE MYSTERIES

very day detectives ponder mysteries. They find clues and solve the cases.

In this book you will read seven strange mysteries. There are many clues, but there is no weapon; there is no stolen money; in fact, there is no crime at all. And the author does not know the answers. Nobody does.

What kind of mysteries are these?

All of the mysteries in this book are about the

human body and the freaky things that can happen to it. Each of the stories is true. You will read about people who burst into flame, develop wounds without being injured, or suddenly die in their sleep.

Scientists are like detectives. They study these cases and try to explain them. You are the detective now. Read about the most bizarre things that have ever happened to the human body.

One
THE
FIRE CURSE

- The ashes of a sixty-eight–year-old Philadelphia woman are found in her room.
  Her shoes and part of her body remain.
  A newspaper lying only two feet away
  from her ashes is not even singed.
- A meter reader enters the basement of
  a ninety-two-year-old retired doctor.
  He sees light blue smoke and discovers
  a pile of ashes on the dirt floor. A hole
  has burned through the bathroom's

floor boards above. Upstairs he finds a piece of leg from the knee down.

■ A man says good night to his mother. When he returns to her apartment in the morning, he finds a gruesome mess. His mother's skull, the size of a baseball, lies among a blackened circle of debris. Her spine has melted. Greasy soot covers the ceiling, but there is no sign of fire elsewhere in the room.

alled spontaneous human combustion, or SHC, cases of humans who have burned to death for no understandable reason have fascinated people for centuries. In SHC a human body mysteriously begins burning without any apparent source of fire. Scientists do not know why this happens.

The first recorded case of spontaneous human combustion occurred in Paris, France, in 1673. The remains of a man who drank heavily were found heaped on a straw bed. His skull and finger bones lay among the ashes. The straw bed did not burn.

For a long time, many people did not believe spontaneous human combustion really happened. They said the man in Paris had alcohol in

his body, the alcohol caught fire from a spark somewhere, and the body burned. We know today that events could not happen this way.

In the nineteenth century, the chemist Baron Justus von Liebig conducted experiments with alcohol. After soaking flesh in alcohol, he lit it with a flame. The alcohol burned awhile, but the bluish flame went out as the alcohol evaporated. This kind of fire is not hot enough to burn a body into ashes.

Throughout history people have had doubts about other cases, too. Some thought a cigarette could have fallen onto a victim's clothing. Or maybe a fireplace spark hit a chair, and then the chair burned with the victim sitting on it. SH was just too impossible to be believed. While is true that some of the victims smoked or next to a fireplace, we know some facts show these explanations are too simple.

When a corpse is cremated, the over reach very high temperatures. The heated for ninety minutes at 2200 degr enheit. Then it must stay at 1800 degr other sixty to one hundred fifty min at these high temperatures, the bo

reduce to ashes. The leftover bones must still be crushed.

Even the worst house fire would not be greater than 1500 degrees Fahrenheit. So if a SHC victim had been trapped in a house fire, he or she wouldn't have become a pile of ashes. The fire wouldn't have been hot enough.

On the other hand, some people say that a smoldering fire, if given enough time, can destroy a body without damaging nearby objects. Sometimes hours or days pass before the victims are discovered in their homes. High temperatures are necessary only if the body must be destroyed quickly.

Other facts suggest that SHC victims could not have burned in an ordinary fire. When flesh burns, a strong, foul odor spreads everywhere. In most cases of spontaneous human combustion, however, there is no bad odor.

In addition, under the high heat needed to destroy the tissue, a head would not shrink as sometimes happens in SHC. Dr. Wilton Krogman, a bone specialist, conducted experiments in which he burned the heads from dead bodies donated to science. The high heat always destroyed the soft tissue in the skull and caused

the head to burst open. "I've never known an exception to this rule," Dr. Krogman stated.

There is another very curious feature of SHC victims. The torso may burn to ashes while the limbs remain untouched. Investigating an unusual death on January 6, 1980, retired policeman John Heymer entered a home in Gwent County, Wales. He reported, "On the floor about one meter from the hearth was a pile of ashes . . . Emerging from the ashes were a pair of human feet clothed in socks. The feet were attached to short lengths of lower leg, encased in trouser leg bottoms. The feet and socks were undamaged . . . Of the torso and arms nothing remained but ash. Opposite the feet was a blackened skull."

This course of action is the exact opposite of ordinary burning, where fire usually scorches the arms and legs first, working its way inward. Like a log burning in the fireplace, the outer parts heat up first because they are the most exposed to the fire. Could people undergoing spontaneous human combustion burn from the inside out?

Perhaps the most mysterious question about SHC is: Why are nearby items untouched? A

(Photo provided by Topham Picture Library)

The ashy
remains of Ms. E. M.,
age sixty-nine, found
dead of "preternatural
combustibility"
in West London,
January 29, 1958.
Although from the
position of her body
it appears she may
have simply fallen
into the fireplace,
an ordinary wood,
gas, or coal fire
is not hot enough
to reduce a human body to ash.
Notice too the wooden chair, rags, and other combustible objects close
to the fireplace which show no signs of being burned or scorched.

tremendous amount of heat is needed to damage the human body in the ways just described. Why haven't buildings burned down? No one knows. Is another force at work? If so, what?

Throughout the ages, many people have offered explanations. An eighteenth-century idea was that particles in the blood bump into each other. The friction causes heat, which starts a fire. In the nineteenth century some people thought that spontaneous human combustion happened to drunkards as a punishment from God. Others said that the alcohol itself decomposed into combustible gases.

Another theory suggested that large amounts of body fat burn like a candle, with the clothes acting as a wick. However, although many victims have been overweight, others have been thin.

Recently the explanations have become more creative. The theory of "geomagnetic fluctuations" claims that changes in the earth's magnetic fields cause people to ignite. Another modern explanation blames too much phosphorus in the body. It is true that living things store energy as bonds between chemicals. Do certain conditions cause an uncontrolled chemical re-action?

Still another theory says that the intense burn-ing comes from a sudden burst of energy like the ones a microwave oven produces. And where does this energy come from? Each atom, the the-ory goes, may have a tiny particle called a pyro-tron. The pyrotrons (as yet unconfirmed) go haywire in a subatomic chain reaction within the body.

To date, no one has been able to prove or dis-prove any of these theories. The best way to in-vestigate something is by doing experiments under controlled conditions. But scientists are not able to study SHC this way. They only hear about a case after it has already happened. Then they must rely on reports from on-the-spot wit-nesses or people who discover victims after the fact. Information like this is not always reliable.

Who are the victims of spontaneous human combustion? How are they different from other people? Again, there can be no firm statements. Since the 1700s there have been about two hun-dred recorded cases. Males and females are struck in roughly equal numbers. SHC victims have been fat and skinny, smokers and

Incendis Corporis Humani Spontaneis, the classic text on spontaneous combustion in human beings, was published in 1763 and was the first scientific study of this phenomenon.

SPECIMEN PATHOLOGICO-MEDICUM
INAUGURALE

DE

INCENDIIS CORPORIS HUMANI SPONTANEIS.

QUOD,

FAVENTE SUMMO NUMINE,

Ex Auctoritate MAGNIFICI RECTORIS

D. DAVIDIS VAN ROYEN,

MEDICINAE DOCTORIS. BOTANICES IN ACAD.
LUGD. BAT. PROFESSORIS ORDINARII:

NEC NON

Amplissimi SENATUS ACADEMICI *Consensu,*
& *Nobilissimae* FACULTATIS MEDICAE *Decreto,*

PRO GRADU DOCTORATUS,

Summisque in MEDICINA Honoribus & Privilegiis
rité ac legitimé consequendis,

Eruditorum Examini submittit

IONAS DUPONT,
AMST. BAT.

Ad diem 16. Decembris M. D. CC. LXIII. *H. L. Q. S.*

Intima pars homini vero flagravit ad ossa:
Flagravit stomacho flamma, ut fornacibus intus.
LUCRET.

LUGDUNI BATAVORUM,

Apud THEODORUM HAAK, Bibliop.

nonsmokers, heavy drinkers and teetotalers. There is no single characteristic that sets the SHC victim apart.

Do some people become so old and lonely that they no longer want to live? Do their bodies self-destruct? Many victims have been elderly persons who lived alone. The oldest victim was 114 years old. But there are reports of young and lively victims, including a teenager who burst into flames while dancing in a room full of other people. The youngest recorded victim was a four-month-old baby.

Whether spontaneous human combustion actually occurs is still debated. Some people object to the word *spontaneous* because candles, pipes, and cigarettes found near many victims could have started the fires. But no one has yet come up with a logical explanation that can be proved. SHC is still a medical mystery.

Two
FIREWALKERS

I n the Greek village of Ayia Eleni a special day has come. Today is May 21, the festival of Saints Constantine and Helen.

Thousands of people have gathered outdoors; many are visitors. There is a clearing in the center of the crowd. Inside the clearing is a cone-shaped pile of logs six feet high.

As dusk falls, a man shouts, "Light the fire!"

Someone brings a burning candle and lights the wood. The logs burn brightly, slowly collapsing into a big mound of flaming pieces and red-hot coals.

Inside a building, a dozen men and women have been dancing. They have danced all afternoon accompanied by music played on a drum and a lira, an instrument with three strings. They sing sad songs.

Now these people move outside, carrying icons, religious pictures painted on wood.

As the sound of the music reaches the crowd, the men tending the fire take long poles and spread the coals flat. The coals form an oval bed about 9 feet wide, 24 feet long, and an inch or so deep.

The barefoot dancers move toward the glowing coals. For a few minutes, they dance around the edges. The coals hiss. Suddenly a woman wearing a blue dress runs across the fire. She holds an icon of Saint Constantine high above her head. The crowd gasps in amazement.

Soon the other dancers go into the fire. They run, dance, and hop on the coals. Huge clouds of sparks rise up. One man scoops up coals in his hand. He throws them into the air. One woman kneels at the edge of the fire. She slaps the coals

(Photo by John Demos/Aperion, courtesy of Princeton University Press)

Anastenarides cross the fire unharmed.

with her hands and shouts, "May it turn to ashes!"

The dancing continues until only ashes remain. Amazingly, no one is hurt.

The people in this ceremony are called Anastenarides. They believe that Saint Constantine protects them from harm. Firewalking occurs in other places, too. People firewalk in India, Spain, Bulgaria, Fiji, Sri Lanka, and even the United States.

What is happening here? Why don't the Anastenarides and other firewalkers get burned?

Before they dance on the coals, firewalkers prepare carefully. They pray, chant, and meditate. Sometimes they fast, not eating for a week or two, to purify themselves for their firewalk. When they finally walk on the hot coals, they are in a trance. This trancelike state shields them from pain, some people say.

This might be true, but it doesn't explain why the skin is not damaged. Firewalkers have no burn marks or blisters.

Several theories exist as to why the skin isn't burned during a firewalk. One explanation, called the Leidenfrost effect, says that the thin layer of water vapor, or sweat, on the soles of the feet insulates the skin from the heat of the coals.

However, the protection offered by the Leidenfrost effect is not very great. If it did help, then it would be better to firewalk with wet feet. But experiments have shown that wet feet are no better than dry feet. Wet feet can even be harmful because they allow little pieces of burning wood to stick to the skin.

There is another reason why the Leidenfrost effect can't explain the absence of burns. There are several points where the feet touch the coals. The entire weight of the firewalker presses on these points. At exactly these points, however, there is no protection, because the pressure has forced away the water vapor, and the feet are in direct contact with the coals.

Other people say that it is the ashes that protect the firewalker. They act as insulation between the heat and the skin. However, the lava rocks the Fiji Islanders use to firewalk on produce hardly any ash.

Several scientists have studied firewalking and have done experiments. In 1974, Friedbert Karger went to the Fiji Islands. He took a special kind of paint that changes color with different

(Photo © Jack Fields, provided by Photo Researchers, Inc.)

Firewalkers in the Fiji Islands perform a ceremonial dance.

temperatures. Karger painted the soles of a firewalker's feet. Then the firewalker pranced onto the hot rocks. He walked over the rocks for four seconds. He also stood on top of one rock for seven seconds. The paint on his feet changed to a color that showed that the temperature was 150 degrees Fahrenheit, or less, throughout the walk. The firewalker's feet were not hurt at all.

Next, Karger poured some paint onto the rocks. The rock where the firewalker stood for seven seconds was 600 degrees Fahrenheit. Karger cut a small piece of callused skin from the firewalker's foot and threw it onto the rocks. It burned almost instantly.

In other experiments, scientists using probes in the bed of coals have found much hotter temperatures. The hottest temperature recorded was 1500 degrees Fahrenheit, according to *The Guiness Book of World Records*.

Is firewalking a case of "mind over matter"? Some studies do suggest that the mind can affect how the body responds to heat.

In 1959, scientists hypnotized thirteen healthy people. The scientists told them that one arm was normal. They said the other arm was very painful and sensitive. It would soon be hurt, they said.

Then the scientists applied heat to both arms. The heat was great enough to give a mild burn. Nine of the thirteen people in the study had greater inflammation and damage on the "sensitive" arm.

Later the scientists gave new suggestions to the people. One arm was sensitive; the other arm was numb, they said. Then they measured the skin temperature and other factors. In the numb arm, there was less blood circulation. There was also less bradykinin, a chemical that helps produce inflammation. Reduced blood flow and lower levels of bradykinin act to lessen damage to tissue.

Perhaps a similar thing happens in firewalkers. If hypnosis can cause the body to act this way, would a firewalker's trance do the same thing? Is there natural protection against damage?

In most places around the world, firewalking is part of a religious ceremony. In the United States, however, firewalkers are usually not worshiping God, a saint, or a spirit. They are searching for their true inner self.

These people go to firewalking classes. The teachers claim that people will be happier and healthier if they learn to walk on fire. They will have the self-confidence and power needed to overcome problems and even cure illnesses. Students must pay hundreds of dollars for the classes.

In order to firewalk, you must tap the hidden powers of the mind, the teachers say. Skeptics say that this is nonsense, and they have formed groups to disprove claims like this. They say that there is a logical explanation for why people can walk over hot coals and that there can't be anything extraordinary about firewalking if everybody can do it.

One man who thinks he has an explanation is physicist Bernard J. Leikind. A physicist deals with the properties of substances, rather than living things. Leikind's explanation does not involve the mind or the body at all.

Temperature and heat are two different things. Heat is what burns, not temperature. Leikind compares firewalking to what happens to a loaf of bread in the oven. After the oven temperature has stabilized and the bread has baked, the bread and the oven shelf both have the same temperature. You can touch the bread for a second or two without getting burned. Touching the metal shelf, however, causes an instant burn.

Metal is able to hold a lot of heat. It is also a good conductor of heat. This means the heat can pass quickly from the metal surface to another surface. The heat passes to your hand and burns you.

The loaf of bread, however, holds less heat and is a poor conductor. It cannot pass heat to your hands as quickly as the metal can. Therefore, you can safely touch the bread.

Leikind says that hot coals, like bread, are poor conductors of heat. Whether the skin burns depends on how long the firewalker's feet are touching the coals.

Some scientists who believe this explanation have tried firewalking themselves. They do not chant, they do not meditate, and they do not think "cool moss, cool moss" as some firewalking teachers suggest. One group of skeptics even walked across the coals thinking "hot rocks, hot rocks."

The scientists have been successful most of the time. But sometimes they have been burned. The reason, they say, is that their skin touched

(Photo provided by Woodfin Camp & Associates, Inc.)

Students of Anthony Robbins's mind-control course, which teaches
firewalking without pain, walk on burning coals.

the coals long enough to burn—longer than one or two seconds.

Maybe there isn't just one explanation for firewalking. Maybe several factors work together. What do you think?

Three
THE
WOUNDS OF
CHRIST

orld War II had ended. Many countries in Europe were in ruins. In the little village of Konnersreuth, Germany, American soldiers gathered around a bleeding woman.

The woman had not been injured in a battle. She had not been in a prison camp. In fact, her wounds had come long before the war started, and they lasted for another seventeen years after the war ended. What were they and how did she get them?

The woman's name was Therese Neumann. She grew up in a German Catholic family who believed in praying to the saints. As a young woman, she dreamed of becoming a missionary in Africa. Unfortunately, a series of accidents ended that dream. While fighting a fire on her family's farm, she fell from a ladder. Several additional falls resulted in paralysis and blindness. Then she had trouble hearing and breathing.

Over the next few years, however, all of these problems went away. By the time she was twenty-eight, she could see, hear, breathe, and walk normally. Therese believed that God cured her. Suddenly a new problem came. Therese developed a mark on the outside of each hand. Over a period of time, a hard, metallike material went through to her palms. The same marks occurred on her feet. These hand and foot marks approximately matched the places where Jesus Christ was nailed to the cross.

Therese Neumann also developed other marks. She had a wound over her heart. Nine wounds circled her head like the crown of thorns that Jesus wore. Her shoulder had a wound. Altogether she had forty-five marks on her body.

Then in 1926, on Good Friday, the date on which Jesus Christ was crucified, blood began to trickle from Therese's wounds, and tears of blood flowed from her eyes.

After Easter, the tears stopped and the wounds no longer bled. But the wounds remained the rest of Therese Neumann's life. They did not become inflamed or infected. Clear membranes covered the spots. Each year on Good Friday, the wounds bled. Therese Neumann lived with these wounds until her death at the age of sixty-four.

These kinds of wounds are called stigmata. Some people believe that they are a special blessing from God because the person with the wounds shares the same suffering as Jesus Christ. Thousands of people, including priests and other religious persons, came to see Therese Neumann. Doctors and scientists studied the stigmata. No one could explain what caused them. No medicine was able to heal the wounds.

Other people have developed stigmata. The first known stigmatist was Saint Francis of Assisi, who lived from 1182(?) to 1226. His hand and

Therese Neumann showing stigmata on her hands.

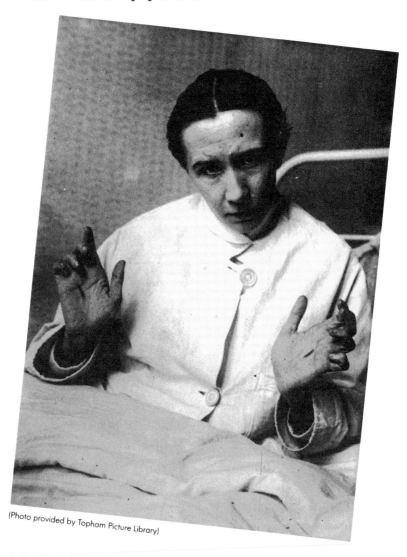

(Photo provided by Topham Picture Library)

foot wounds also had nails formed by the flesh itself. In the palms of his hands and the upper side of his feet, the heads of the nails were round and black. On the opposite side, the points of the nails were long and bent over.

Since the time of Saint Francis, there have been over 300 known stigmatists. Padre Pio was the first stigmatist in the twentieth century. He was an Italian priest who developed circular marks on the fronts and backs of his hands and feet. His wounds stayed with him for fifty years.

When Padre Pio died in 1968, another strange thing happened. The wounds suddenly disappeared. The skin became soft and elastic. There were no scars or other signs of bleeding. Dr. Sala, the physician who examined Padre Pio, said, "Such symptoms and behavior . . . must be considered as outside of every type of a clinical nature. They have an 'extra-natural' character."

Not all cases of stigmatization are mysterious. Sometimes people try to fake the wounds to get attention. In the sixteenth century, a nun in Portugal painted marks on her hands and feet, then claimed the marks were nail wounds.

Even today, some people try to fool others. They pretend to see God or claim to have special

Saint Francis receives the stigmata.

(Painting by Richartz Wallraf, courtesy of New York Public Library Picture Collection)

powers such as healing the sick. In 1986 a Montreal man claimed his statue of the Virgin Mary cried tears of blood. A laboratory analysis showed something quite different. The man had mixed beef and pork fat with his own blood. In a warm room, the mixture softened and dripped down the statue.

Other times people hurt themselves on purpose. They poke themselves with knives or other sharp objects to create the kinds of wounds that Christ had.

Some people do get marks and bruises without being injured. The wounds are real, but they are not true stigmata, even though they might sometimes bleed. Dr. Oscar D. Ratnoff is a hematologist in Cleveland, Ohio. A hematologist is a doctor who specializes in blood. Dr. Ratnoff has studied more than 100 cases of bruises and bleeding that occur by themselves. He believes that many of these cases are psychogenic—the body produces these marks because the person is under a lot of stress. Other studies have shown that thinking and suggestion can produce changes in the skin.

There are several ways to tell if stigmata are false. The wounds last for only a few weeks, not years. They lie on the surface of the skin instead of penetrating deeply into the body. The wounds do not cause very much pain. The wounds might appear or disappear through hypnosis. The wounds can be changed with medicine. Infection or pus might form. And fakers, unlike true stigmatists, often try to show off to others and draw attention to the wounds.

These things don't happen with real stigmata. No chemicals or medicine can heal the wounds, but they don't become infected either. There is often a pleasant smell like perfume coming from the wounds.

The stigmatist is well-adjusted and does not try to show off. He or she may even try to hide the wounds. Therese Neumann, Saint Francis, and Padre Pio all had stable personalities. Many people knew them for a long time and did not notice any strange behavior. When psychiatrists observe stigmatists and perform tests they do not find any personality problems.

True stigmata are very painful. The pain never leaves. Sometimes, however, people have the pain but not the marks. If certain places on the skin are touched, the person feels pain. These kinds of wounds are called invisible stigmata.

Sister Maria Fidelis Weiss, who died in Bavaria (part of Germany) in 1923, had invisible stigmata. Other times a stigmatist may have visible wounds for a long time. Then the marks suddenly disappear, but the pain remains.

There is an interesting feature of hand stigmata. We know some facts about crucifixion. Many religious pictures show Jesus Christ nailed to the cross. The nails go through the palms of his hands. A real crucifixion could not happen this way.

If someone were nailed to a cross through the palms, the weight of the body would create a lot of pressure, causing the nails to rip right through the palms. The body would fall down. But if the nails went through the wrists, the body would stay in place.

Dr. Pierre Barbet tried each of these methods on a cadaver, the body of a person who has died. When he nailed a cadaver through the palms, the body ripped loose.

We have another piece of evidence to show how a crucifixion works. The Shroud of Turin is an ancient linen cloth. The cloth has the image of a naked man in its fibers. Some people believe this cloth was used to wrap Jesus Christ's body after his crucifixion.

In 1988, the shroud was studied with up-to-date scientific procedures. Although the study could not prove or disprove that the cloth was used to cover Jesus, most people do agree that the Shroud of Turin covered the body of a crucified man. During Christ's time, death by crucifixion was a common form of punishment for crimes such as robbery.

The images of the man's hands on the Shroud show the nail wounds in the wrists, not in the palms. But Therese Neumann's hand wounds were in her palms. In fact, most stigmatists' hand wounds occur in the palms. Why?

The stigmatists know that their hand wounds do not match Christ's exactly. They say that the location of their wounds has a personal meaning to them. The wounds come where they envision them. Indeed, most stigmatists' marks match wounds that they have seen in pictures while praying.

Therese Neumann's other stigmata occurred in the proper positions. Her side wound occurred between the fifth and sixth ribs on the right side. An opening came through to the back.

Father Peter M. Rinaldi holds a replica of the Shroud of Turin. The shroud, venerated by Roman Catholics for 600 years as the burial cloth of Jesus, has been subjected to science's most modern investigative techniques in efforts to solve the mystery of the image of a crucified man on a fourteen-foot linen strip. The shroud is kept at the Cathedral of Turin.

(Photo by Jack Balletti, provided by UPI/Bettmann)

The location of this wound is identical to the image on the Shroud of Turin.

Are stigmata still occurring today? There are several reports of living stigmatists in Italy, Germany, and France. Father James Bruse is a priest who lives in Lake Ridge, Virginia. In December 1991, he complained of sharp pains in his wrists. Later, blood seeped from his skin. He wore wristbands to hide his wrists. In August 1992, the bleeding stopped.

This period of time is very short. Possible cases of stigmata should be studied over many years. Doctors and psychiatrists should examine the person. An illness or a hoax must be considered.

Using modern techniques and laboratory tests, doctors studied a woman for several months in 1975. The twenty-three-year-old Mexican-American attended church regularly and prayed constantly. Doctors witnessed her palms bleeding through unbroken skin. The tissue under the skin looked normal. The doctors collected the blood and sent it to the lab. The lab reported a normal composition. The blood was compared to blood drawn through the woman's veins, and the samples matched each other perfectly. During the study, the doctors measured other things such as brain waves, pulse, and breathing. They could not draw any conclusions. Some people said that the woman's two-year-old baby also had stigmata, but the doctors did not see this.

What causes stigmata? No one knows. Some doctors have suggested a viral infection or allergic reaction. If the mind alone can produce the wounds, science doesn't know how.

Although most stigmata mimic the wounds of Christ, reports of stigmata occur in other religions also. Hindu lore contains accounts of stigmatists. In the Muslim religion, Muhammad was in a battle for the spread of his faith. Some stigmata imitate his battle wounds.

Are stigmata real? What causes them? What do they mean? You decide.

Four
HAIRY WILDMEN

O n a dark, lonely road in central China, a Jeep bounced along swiftly. As it turned a sharp corner, the vehicle cast its headlights on a creature standing in the road. The driver stopped the Jeep, and five men got out. They couldn't believe what they saw.

In the beam of the headlights stood a furry creature about six feet tall. He had thick thighs shorter than the lower part of his leg. His arms hung below his knees. He had big hands with fingers about six inches long. His feet were twelve inches long. Suddenly the creature ran from the headlights and disappeared into the woods.

The next day, the men sent a telegram to the Academy of Sciences in Beijing. They said that they had just seen a *ye ren* — a wildman.

There are many stories about big, hairy creatures that live in the mountain forests of China's Shennongjia region. Poems written over two thousand years ago contain descriptions of mountain beasts. Seven hundred years later, a history writer reported that a group of hairy men lived in the forests. During the 1700s, another poet told a tale of monkeylike creatures. Many paintings have images of the *ye ren*. Their pictures even appear on ancient money.

Until 1976, however, most people thought these were just stories. They did not think a real wildman could exist. When the men in the Jeep told about their experience, the Academy of Sciences became interested and began to investigate. Soon hundreds of reports came from farmers and other people living in central China.

They said that they had seen mysterious creatures, too.

Thirty-three-year-old commune leader Pang Gensheng talked about the day he saw a hairy wildman. In October 1977, he went to chop wood on the side of a hill. He looked up and saw something coming toward him.

"He was about seven feet tall, with shoulders wider than a man's, a sloping forehead, deep-set eyes, and a bulbous nose with slightly upturned nostrils," Pang recalls. "His eyes were black. His hair was dark brown, more than a foot long, and hung loosely over his shoulders. His whole face, except for the nose and ears, was covered with short hairs."

The creature moved closer and closer. Pang backed against a stone cliff and raised his ax. Each of them stood motionless.

"Then I groped for a stone and threw it at him," Pang says. "It hit him in the chest. He uttered several howls and rubbed the spot with his left hand. Then he turned left and leaned against a tree, then walked away slowly toward the bottom of the gully. He kept making a mumbling sound."

The Academy of Sciences organized a team to

look for the wildmen. More than a hundred people spent two years searching the forests. They checked all the areas where sightings had been reported. They did not find any wildmen, but they found some interesting clues.

In one area, the investigators found footprints that measured approximately four inches wide in front and two inches wide at the back. The big toe was separated from the four other toes. Occurring in single file, the footprints were approximately two to three feet apart.

The team went to one area where several witnesses said they had seen hairy creatures, including a mother and child. The researchers found piles of feces. They collected the hardened feces and analyzed the contents in the lab.

The feces contained pieces of fruit skins and wild nuts but no animal parts. The scientists said that the size of the droppings and the size of the food particles were too small for a bear or hoofed animal. A carnivorous (meat-eating) animal could not have produced the feces. And the feces were not like human feces. They concluded that the feces were most like those of the primate order, to which apes and monkeys belong.

The most important evidence came after a

woman reported seeing a hairy creature scratching its back against a tree. Gong Yulan ran from the forest crying, "A wildman! A wildman!"

When the scientists looked for the creature, they could not find it, but they did find several pieces of dark brown hair on the tree trunk. They collected the strands and sent them to Beijing for analysis. Scientists looked at the hair under a microscope. Based on the shape and nature of the hair, it could not have come from a bear. The hair was most like that of the primates.

Dr. Frank E. Poirier, an American professor at Ohio State University, became interested in the possibility that wildmen might exist. In 1990, he traveled to China to look at the evidence. The Chinese had collected more hairs from bushes, trees, and the ground. Their equipment and tests were more modern than in 1976.

Chinese scientists at Huadong University in Shanghai used an electron scanning microscope to look at the hairs. This kind of microscope can reveal much more detail than an ordinary microscope can. The scientists saw the inside as well as the outside of the hairs. The hairs were typical of primates in general but not of any known species.

"Have You Seen It, the Wildman?" read a sign posted by scientists in a village in Sichuan Province, China. It asked for information about evidence of a humanlike primate.

(International Society of Cryptozoology, courtesy of *New York Times*)

At Fudan University, also in Shanghai, scientists used a particle accelerator to determine the chemical makeup of the hairs. The ratio of iron to zinc is unique for each species. Again, the results were puzzling. The ratio of iron to zinc was similar to that found in primates but higher than any known species, including man.

"This is most exciting and unexpected news," Dr. Poirier said. "For the very first time there is scientific evidence for the possible existence of an unknown primate."

Is it possible that an undiscovered species of apeman exists? It is true that some kinds of animals once thought to be extinct are actually alive in remote places on earth. We know from fossils that a giraffelike animal called an okapi lived millions of years ago. In 1901 scientists saw for the first time a live okapi in an African jungle. Shorter than a giraffe and lacking a long neck, the shy animal comes out at night to feed. The okapi uses its long tongue and flexible lips to pick leaves from trees and bushes.

Many rare plant and animal species live in central China today. The dove tree and the Chinese tulip tree grow here. The giant panda lives here. The panda also lived here 2 million years ago, side by side with a big manlike ape known as *Gigantopithecus*. Are the hairy wildmen descended from this ape? The fossilized bones of the ape are massive and fit the descriptions that eyewitnesses give of the wildmen. If the giant panda and other kinds of animals survived in this region, could *Gigantopithecus* have survived also? One theory says so.

Another theory says that the *ye ren* are atavisms—throwbacks to an earlier form of the species. Genes, which determine body characteristics like eye color and hairiness, come from each parent. If they combine a certain way, the characteristic appears in the child. So, for example, a mother and father might each have a "hairy gene." By itself, the gene does not cause hairiness. However, if each parent passed a hairy gene to a child, the child would then have two hairy genes. Together, these two genes might cause the child to be hairy. Some people think the hairy wildmen might have originated this way.

Hairy babies do exist in China. In 1978, Yu Zhenhuan was born with hair covering his entire body and face. His parents and sister are not hairy. The Academy of Sciences knows of only

Two-year-old Liu Hua, a hairy girl from northeast China's Liaoning
Province.

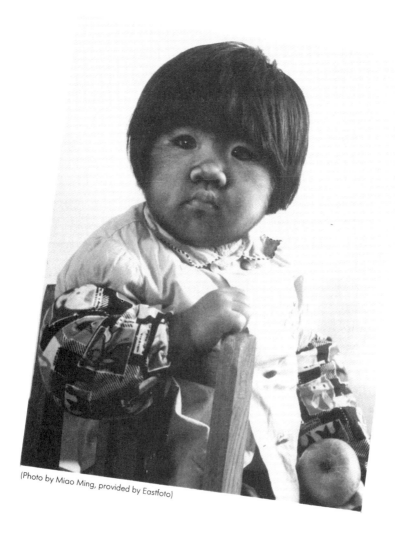

(Photo by Miao Ming, provided by Eastfoto)

nineteen similar cases living in China. All of these people have hair that parts on the sides of the body and is thicker at the center of the back and stomach. The hair forms whorls at various points. Other primates do not have this kind of pattern.

These hairy people are normal in other ways. They eat and develop normally and are just as intelligent as other people. Despite this fact, hairy people have been rejected for centuries. Not having very much body hair themselves, the Chinese find it objectionable. In the past parents sometimes killed hairy babies or just left them in the forest to die.

Those who support the atavism theory think that some of these hairy outcasts may have survived. Through the ages, they had children of their own and developed colonies. However, this does not explain their size. Eyewitnesses often say that the wildmen are seven feet tall. People who believe this theory say that perhaps bigger, stronger creatures survived in the harsh mountains.

Scientists still do not know exactly how a hairy baby grows so much hair. There are several ideas about this, too. Perhaps the genes fail

Hairy child Yu Zhenhuan from Liaoning Province at two years old.

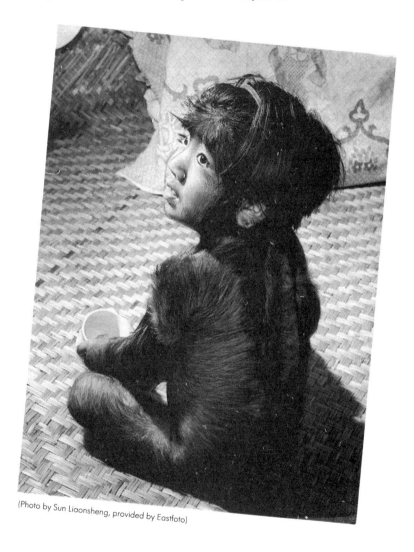

(Photo by Sun Liaonsheng, provided by Eastfoto)

to control hair growth. All human bodies are actually covered with tiny hairs, but most of them never grow. All humans, both male and female, also secrete a female hormone, which stops hair from growing in certain places on the body. Perhaps the hairy people lack this female hormone.

There are many unanswered questions about hairy babies and about the *ye ren*. Until a hairy creature is actually seen and studied by scientists, no one can answer these questions. Maybe someday you will travel to China, see a hairy wildman, and help to solve this mystery.

Five
SLEEPING DEATH

t was an ordinary Friday evening for Ying Yang. The twenty-seven-year-old California factory worker ate dinner, talked with his family, and went to bed. During the night, however, something strange happened. He began to make loud, gurgling sounds in his sleep. His wife sat up and tried to wake Ying Yang. Unable to rouse her husband, she called an ambulance.

Before dawn, Ying Yang was dead.

Doctors performed an autopsy; they cut open the body and examined the heart, lungs, stomach, and other parts. Nothing unusual was found. They could not find the cause of death. Ying Yang had been perfectly healthy and had not taken any drugs.

Since 1977, over 140 similar deaths have occurred in the United States. They have all been mysterious. All but one of the victims were men. Most of the men were between twenty-five and forty-five years old. Ninety-eight percent of the deaths occurred between 10:00 P.M. and 8:00 A.M. Newspapers and journals have called the strange deaths by several names: Night Death, Sudden Unexplained Death Syndrome (SUDS), Sudden Unexpected Nocturnal Death Syndrome (SUNDS), and other variations.

What else do these deaths have in common? Like Ying Yang, the victims were not born in the United States. They came to America from countries in Southeast Asia including Vietnam, Cambodia, Thailand, and Laos.

The people most at risk are members of the Hmong tribe, who lived in the mountains of Laos. During the Vietnam War in the 1960s and

1970s, they helped the United States fight the North Vietnamese and the Pathet Lao Communists. The Hmong were fierce fighters and loyal friends. They hid U.S. pilots who were shot down.

After U.S. troops left, the Communists tried to kill the Hmong for helping the Americans. They dropped bombs. Some Hmong say that they dropped poisonous chemicals too. The Hmong people escaped from Laos and went to refugee camps in Thailand. From there, many of them came to the United States. Since the mid-1970s, about 97,000 Hmong have settled across the country.

The Hmong's troubles did not end, however. They were lonely and homesick. Life in big cities was very different from that of the rural mountain villages where they once lived proudly. Unable to speak English, they could not find good jobs. As the number of Hmong living in the United States increased, so did the number of mysterious sleeping deaths.

One of these deaths occurred in 1982 after Nao Shua Thao and his wife, Yang Cher, brought their four children to Chicago. New refugees must get a medical checkup. No serious problems were found. However, doctors found a small enlargement in Yang Cher's neck and recommended an operation to remove it.

Yang Cher was frightened and did not want to have the operation. Unaware that someone can refuse medical treatment, Nao Shua forced his wife to go to the hospital. That night in the hospital, Yang Cher had a dream. She and Nao Shua were splitting up their money. She knew what the dream meant. Either the husband or wife would die soon.

The next day Yang Cher told her husband about the dream. She begged to come home. He tried to comfort his wife, then went home himself. Nao Shua shared his wife's concerns, and now he was upset and frightened, too. He went back to the hospital to see Yang Cher once more before the operation.

When he got to the hospital, visiting hours were over. A nurse turned him away. Nao Shua found another entrance and went up to Yang Cher's floor. But he could not speak English, and another nurse made him leave. Now he was terrified that Yang Cher would die and he would never see her again.

Depressed and anxious, Nao Shua went home

Nao Shua Thao, right, is the fifty-ninth recorded case of nocturnal death
to occur among Southeast Asian refugees in the United States.

(Photo by David Falconer)

again. The children snuggled up to him and they all fell asleep. In the middle of the night one of the children heard Nao Shua making loud groans. But the little boy fell back asleep.

When morning came, everybody but Nao Shua woke up. He was dead. The children's uncle came over and took care of them. Yang Cher's operation was a success, but she did not find out about her husband's death until she came home three days later.

The number of strange deaths continued across the country. Wherever the refugees settled—California, Oregon, Minnesota—some of them died suddenly in their sleep. In 1981, the Centers for Disease Control in Atlanta, Georgia, began to investigate. They collected information about the deaths and tried to solve the mystery.

In each case, the autopsies showed no abnormal marks or changes in the victims' hearts, lungs, or other major organs. Many of the Hmong blamed the deaths on the "yellow rain," the nerve gases and other chemicals that the Communists dropped on Laos. But the bodies of the victims had no traces of poisonous chemicals. Most of the victims had never come in contact with the yellow rain. Even if they had been exposed, the toxins would kill instantly, not years later. And the chemicals would have affected women as well as men.

One theory is that the deaths may be linked to a virus, a germ that causes illness. For example, common colds are caused by viruses. Perhaps the refugees caught a virus at the U.S. immigration centers and the disease weakened them. However, there is no evidence from the autopsies that indicates this might have happened.

Another theory suggests that the Hmong people have weak hearts. But studies show that their hearts and blood vessels are in better condition than those of most Americans. Still another thought is that the Hmong died from sleep apnea. A person with sleep apnea has very restless sleep and an irregular heartbeat, snores loudly, and actually stops and starts breathing many times during the night. However, the sleeping death victims did not have these symptoms.

Some researchers have looked into the possibility that food played a role in the deaths. They examined the victims' last meals but did not find any clues. Ronald Munger of the University of Iowa's medical school studied the problem. After he examined Hmong in the refugee camps in

Thailand, he found that they lack the vitamin thiamine in their food. But there is no proof that this could cause the sudden deaths.

Another investigator wondered about the long-term effects of diet. Have the Hmong's eating habits changed since they came to the United States? Could the changes explain the deaths? He came up with nothing.

Similar deaths have occurred in healthy Thai men who worked in Singapore, Malaysia. The health officials looked at their cooking methods. The construction workers used plastic pipes to steam rice. When plastic burns, it can give off poisonous gases. However, the Thai men did not heat the pipes enough to produce these gases.

Everywhere the medical detectives looked turned out to be a dead end. They checked the possibility of allergies, epilepsy, and other diseases. "We drew a complete blank," says James Essling, an investigator in Minnesota. "In each case, we asked ourselves what they had died from and the answer was 'Nothing.' "

Is it possible the refugees were frightened to death? Can stress and fear kill?

Maybe. Doctors at Harvard Medical School studied 117 patients who had almost died but were revived. Their hearts had stopped entirely or had arrhythmia—abnormal heartbeats—which can lead to death. Twenty-four of the patients had just been through extremely stressful situations that day. Fifteen of these people had the problem less than an hour before the arrhythmia started. Several had nightmares. Before the attacks, their hearts had been normal.

In another study, doctors looked at fifteen victims of violent crimes who had died, although the injuries from their attacks were minor. Dr. Marilyn Cebelin of Case Western Reserve University reported that their hearts had a unique pattern of damage, unlike what occurs from a heart attack. It was more like the damage seen in laboratory animals placed under stress. She said that the body's reaction to fear destroyed the heart cells.

"There was no other reason for these people to die," she said. "The evidence indicates that the stress caused by fear can provoke lethal changes in the heart muscle."

The autopsies showed bright red patches of dead cells among the live cells. The dead cells disrupt nerve cells that control beating. If the heart can't beat smoothly, it may fail, and the person may die.

The fear that the crime victims experienced was very intense. It is different from the kind of fear you might have while watching a horror movie. In that situation, you are in control. You could simply leave the theater or turn off the TV if you wanted to.

Could the Hmong refugees have had scary dreams just before they died? The refugees died peacefully, and there was no screaming, kicking, or other restless movements that usually come with nightmares. However, scientists have made some interesting discoveries about sleep itself that may shed light on these mysterious sleeping deaths.

Sleep occurs in different stages. Most dreams and nightmares occur toward morning during one of the REM (rapid eye movement) stages. The body has had time to adjust to the anxiety of the bad dream. Breathing and heartbeat may change slightly. People usually remember their nightmares.

We now know that there is another kind of sleep event called a night terror, which occurs earlier in the night, during a deeper stage of sleep. They happen suddenly. People don't usually remember a night terror, but when they do, they report the intense panic of being crushed, smothered, or chased. During the night terror, the nervous system runs wild. Breathing increases dramatically. The heart pounds rapidly. The sleeper awakens with a scream but then quickly returns to deep sleep.

Not everyone has night terrors. Some children have them but they are harmless and do not usually occur after the age of eight. If an adult has night terrors, they increase during times of stress. The episodes are worse if the person has a lot of bottled-up anger.

The Hmong refugees had a lot of stress when they lived in Southeast Asia. The stress didn't go away when they came to the United States. Perhaps the refugees had night terrors.

One Hmong refugee survived the sleeping death. An emergency crew arrived quickly at Ge Xiong's house in Seattle and gave him CPR (cardiopulmonary resuscitation). His life was saved. He doesn't remember anything about his sleep that night. However, he remembers a similar attack five years earlier: "You want to listen, you can't hear. You want to speak, you are dumb.

Ge Xiong, a Hmong man from Seattle, is the only documented case of a Southeast Asian refugee who suffered a nocturnal attack and survived.

(Photo by David Falconer)

You want to call out, you cannot. You feel you are dying, dying. You want to run away." Was he having a night terror?

The number of sleeping deaths was highest during 1981 and 1982. Now there are many fewer deaths. Less than five cases are reported each year. We no longer have very many Southeast Asian refugees coming to this country. The refugees who now live here are adjusting to life in the United States. In 1987 the Centers for Disease Control called off its investigation. Perhaps the sleeping death will remain a medical mystery forever.

Six
RACE AGAINST TIME

enny Vantine grumbles as the nurse wraps a blood pressure cuff around her tiny, frail arm. Blue veins are scattered over the surface of her thin, wrinkled skin. Her hands and feet are cold and clammy. She has lost most of her hair. Her ears stick out; her face looks like a bird's face. She also has arthritis, cataracts, and kidney and liver disease. Penny Vantine is dying of old age.

But Penny is only five years old. She suffers
from Cockayne's syndrome, in which the body
grows old much faster than normal. There are
other similar diseases, such as progeria (Hutch-
inson-Gilford syndrome) and Werner's syndrome. Together, these are called premature
aging diseases. They are all very rare. In all of
recorded history, only about sixty cases of Cockayne's syndrome have occurred worldwide. In
1990, there were only eighteen progeria patients
in the world.

Whether plant or animal, all living things have
a natural life span. For example, a tree might live
to be 500 years old. Humans usually live to be
about seventy-five. As each living thing gets
older, it wears out and dies. We do not know why
this happens or how the process works. In the
premature aging diseases, the victim's body
wears out in a very short period of time. The
aging process runs out of control.

When progeria babies are born, there is no
way of predicting that they will suffer from premature aging. They do not weigh any less than
other babies. "Usually they look pretty normal,"
according to Ted Brown, M.D., an expert on progeria. "Occasionally there are some early signs,

but usually they have normal hair, they look like normal children."

When April Frankland was born, nobody noticed anything unusual. "At six weeks," her mother recalls, "her skin started getting really tough."

After a few months, April's mom knew something was wrong. April didn't gain the amount of weight that other babies her age gain. Not until April was two years old, however, did doctors give the diagnosis of progeria. By this time April's hair began to fall out, including eyebrows and eyelashes. When she appeared on the television talk show "Donahue" at age nine, she wore a wig. Her muscles and bones had stopped growing.

When Mickey Hays appeared on a different "Donahue" show, he was also nine years old. He wore a baseball cap to cover his bald head. His face had lost the thin layer of fat that lies beneath the skin. His eyes bulged outward, and his nose was thin and beaklike.

Mickey looked like an old man but talked and acted like a child. In many respects, he was just a normal fourth grader with lots of friends in school. He enjoyed visiting Disney World. Al-

Mickey Hays, age nine, straddles a large motorcycle at his parents'
Longview, Texas, home. Mickey has progeria, a disease that has
prematurely aged his body to the equivalent of a sixty-five-year-
old man.

(Photo by Mike Gibson, provided by AP/Wide World Photos)

Mickey Hays at age fifteen.

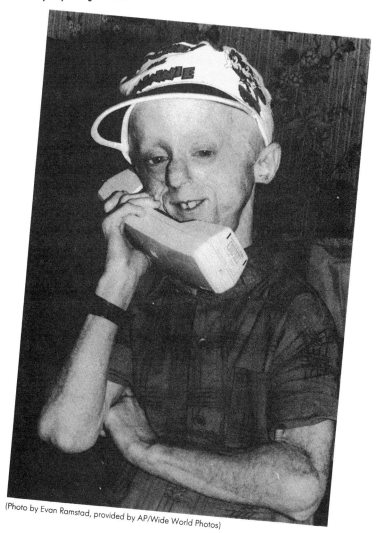

(Photo by Evan Ramstad, provided by AP/Wide World Photos)

though his face and body aged too fast, his mind was like that of a typical nine-year-old.

As people grow old, their brains undergo changes. Thinking and reaction time slows down. Often they become forgetful. These kinds of changes don't happen to progeria patients, according to Dr. Dorothy Villee from Boston Children's Hospital. Like Mickey, most progeria patients have average or above average intelligence. People with Cockayne's syndrome, however, are often born mentally retarded.

There is no cure for any of the premature aging diseases. But the victims can go to school and play and lead otherwise normal lives, however short. Eventually the problems of old age set in, the actual age varying just as it does for normally aged people. Slowly the victims lose their sight until they are totally blind. Hearing loss leads to deafness. Breathing difficulties and heart problems are typical, and the patients soon die from an infection, heart attack, or kidney or liver failure. By the time they have become teenagers, progeria or Cockayne's syndrome patients have lived their entire life span. Only a few patients have lived into their twenties.

The person with Werner's syndrome is a little bit luckier. This condition is called adult progeria, because it does not start until the late teen years. The person might live to be thirty or forty. Like childhood progeria, however, the victim has similar bizarre symptoms, and the disease takes the same bleak path. The patient always ages and dies much younger than is normal.

What causes the premature aging diseases?

Meg Casey, a progeria patient who lived into her twenties, once said, "The only thing absolutely known about progeria today is that nothing is absolutely known about progeria today."

Nevertheless, there are some ideas on what causes premature aging. Scientists do know that it is genetic. This means that it involves DNA (deoxyribonucleic acid), a complex chemical with thousands of components. DNA exists in each of the body's billions of cells. The DNA directs all of the body's functions, including growth and aging. If there is something wrong with the DNA, then one or more of these functions may not work properly. Scientists know exactly which pieces of DNA cause many diseases. But they have not found the piece that causes premature aging.

Each person receives DNA from his or her parents. Therefore, some scientists think that the DNA premature aging victims receive from their parents is unhealthy. There is some evidence to support this idea. In some families, more than one child has progeria. There is one family in which identical twins both have progeria. Identical twins each have exactly the same kind of DNA.

Other scientists, however, do not think that the faulty DNA comes from the parents. They think that the child receives healthy DNA from the mother and father. Then some unknown agent—possibly a drug, radiation, or a pesticide—damages the DNA long before the child is born. This process is called a mutation. As the body's cells divide, the DNA is copied into each new cell. Thus every cell of the body contains the mistake.

Once the body contains faulty DNA, how does it produce the disease? Studies on some patients show that they lack a growth hormone. Growth hormones are necessary for normal growth of muscles and bones. Dr. Ted Brown says, "Most of the children don't weigh more than twenty-five to thirty pounds, occasionally up to forty pounds. And they're usually about three and a half feet tall." Patients treated with the missing growth hormone, however, still do not grow.

On the one hand, the victims of the premature aging diseases do not grow up. On the other hand, they age too fast. We do not know why. And we still do not understand what causes aging in general.

Scientists have conducted some interesting studies comparing the cells of healthy people to those of premature aging victims. Human cells can grow outside the body. We measure the life of these cells by the number of times they double in number. Normal skin cells will double their number approximately fifty times before they die.

Scientists took skin cells from patients suffering from several of the premature aging diseases. They grew the cells in the laboratory. Cells from progeria patients doubled only ten to thirty-two times. Cells from Werner's syndrome patients doubled only about ten times before they died. And cells from Rothmund-Thomson syndrome patients, another premature aging disease, did not double at all.

Next the scientists used a microscope to

(Photo by Eddie Adams, provided by AP/Wide World Photos)

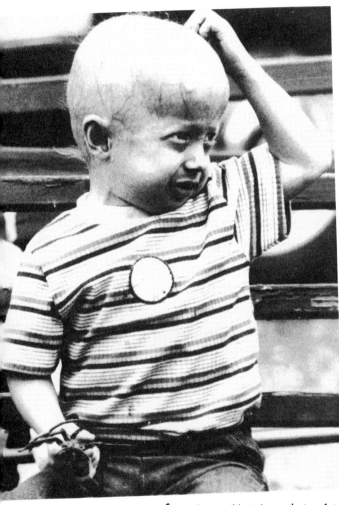

Four-year-old Peedie Snipes *(left)* and Lonnie Carney, two, participate in a gathering of victims of progeria in 1982. Eight progeriacs, their parents, and medical experts gathered to discuss the apparently genetic disorder and to meet socially.

examine the structure of the normal cells and the diseased cells. They looked at the cells early in their growth period and at the end of their life. They saw that normal cells change as they age. Their overall size and shape changes, and the inside of the cells contain different structures. The cells taken from premature aging victims showed the characteristics of old cells even at very young ages.

The scientists made a similar comparison with the chemical makeup of the cells. All cells contain enzymes, substances that guide chemical reactions in the body. For example, the saliva in your mouth contains an enzyme that begins to digest some of the food you eat. As they age, normal cells are unable to break down the old enzymes. These old, inactive enzymes accumulate inside the cell. The scientists found that the cells of premature aging victims contained high amounts of these inactive enzymes.

What do these studies mean? They demonstrate that the problem with premature aging might lie inside each cell of the body. Without proper enzymes, the cells may not be able to respond to outside stress. Scientists believe that these cells may not be able to repair damage to themselves.

Other research is limited. Since there are few patients, there is little money available to study this condition. Stars do not hold telethons to raise money to help these sufferers. The government does not fund any research programs, as it does for diseases such as AIDS. Meanwhile, science struggles with the mystery of why young children grow old before they grow up.

Seven
DOG SENSE

n a large classroom, several dogs sat quietly with their trainers. Their obedience class was over, and they were waiting for a group of disabled people to arrive. The visitors wanted to adopt trained dogs for friendship and help. The dogs could open doors, pick up dropped items, and fetch clothes, among other tasks.

When the visitors came into the room, the dogs watched eagerly, but they remained calm, as they had been taught. They did not try to leave their trainers. However, a three-year-old

German shepherd named Kelly had other ideas. She started panting and whining. She paced back and forth and tugged on her leash. She did not usually act this way.

One by one, the dogs were allowed to meet the new people. They wagged their tails and let the people pet them. When it was Kelly's turn, she went straight to a girl in a wheelchair. She whined and pushed her nose into the girl's hand, but refused to let the girl pet her on the head. Kelly ignored the other people who waited to meet her. The dog trainer told Kelly, "Come." But Kelly remained with the girl and ignored all commands.

Suddenly the girl's face grew pale. Her eyes rolled back and her body shook wildly. Kelly stayed by the girl's side until the attack ended. When the girl finally relaxed, Kelly became herself once again. She obeyed her trainer's commands and let people pet her.

The girl in the wheelchair had just suffered a seizure. She has a disease known as epilepsy. The brain of someone with epilepsy is unable to send electrical signals properly. The dog appeared to know that the girl was going to have a seizure before the girl or anyone else knew.

Several other people have noticed this behavior in their dogs. Based in New York City, The Epilepsy Institute has received about a dozen reports nationwide of dogs who acted strangely before their masters had an epileptic seizure. Might this ability be used to help people?

Epilepsy is not a deadly condition by itself. However, it is a dangerous disease, because the victim cannot control his or her movements during a seizure. The epileptic may lose consciousness and fall, injuring himself or herself. While unconscious, breathing passages might be blocked. The epilepsy victim might even be walking in traffic when a seizure strikes. A dog who warned of an oncoming attack would prevent an epileptic from being in a dangerous situation when a seizure was about to occur. The dog could also signal for help once an attack began. A seizure-alert dog would help the person live a normal, independent life.

This was the goal for Victoria Doroshenko. In 1984 she had a serious car accident that destroyed part of her brain and caused epilepsy. She began to have seizures—as many as twenty-four severe ones each day, with ten smaller ones in between. She would fall often. She couldn't leave her house.

In 1987 Victoria heard about a program at the Washington Correction Center for Women, near Tacoma. The program aims to teach prisoners the skills of boarding, grooming, and training dogs. The trained dogs become aids to the handicapped. The prisoners thought that Harley, a golden retriever, might help Victoria.

On the day that Victoria came to visit, she had a major seizure. Harley ignored his trainer's commands and went to Victoria. He laid down beside her until the attack was over.

"When Vickie started seizuring and Harley went to her and laid down with her, everybody in the room was astounded. The dog was doing what we had hoped he could learn to do. . . . He somehow knew," commented Sue Miller, the dog's trainer.

Harley and Victoria became good friends. Fifteen to forty-five minutes before a seizure came, Harley would bark. He kept her away from dangerous places. With Harley at her side, Victoria could leave her home whenever she wanted without worrying.

One time Victoria had a bad seizure and

Victoria Doroshenko and her companion dog, Harley, who can detect
the onset of an epileptic seizure.

(Photo provided by Victoria Doroshenko)

needed to go to the hospital. She took Harley with her and was resting comfortably. A nearby patient was hooked up to an EEG (electroencephalograph), which records brain waves. Suddenly Harley started barking at the patient.

Doctors and nurses came running. Looking at the EEG, they said nothing was wrong. They said the patient was fine and then left the room. Moments later, the patient had a seizure.

How can Kelly, Harley, and other dogs predict seizures when even the victims don't know that they're coming? There are several ideas about how this happens.

One theory suggests that seizure-alert ability may be part of a dog's natural instincts. An instinct is a behavior that an animal is born with. For example, many birds have the instinct to fly south for the winter. Dogs make nice house pets, but they are related to wolves and once lived in the wild. They traveled together in packs, each pack having a leader. The "packing" instincts ensured that the pack survived and stayed together. In this way, the entire pack contributed to the safety of each member.

When humans adopted dogs as pets, we became part of their pack. Most often, the human took the dominant role, and the dogs looked to the human as the pack leader. If the pack leader is in danger, the dogs' packing instinct would make them try to protect him or her. They would also try to alert other nearby members of the pack. Perhaps an epileptic seizure in a human triggers this kind of protective instinct.

Not all dogs who can predict seizures, however, act protectively. Trainer Sue Miller has seen two dogs who have growled and become fierce. Under normal conditions these dogs acted perfectly fine with people, as well as other dogs and animals. Even when they were around the epilepsy victim, they were friendly and gentle. But as soon as a seizure came, they tried to attack the person, as if they were hunting down prey. Does this kind of behavior come from another type of instinct? A pack of wolves hunting caribou (a kind of deer) does not go after the entire herd. They select one of the weaker caribou. Then they all jump in and attack.

Sue Miller has noticed another interesting thing about the dogs who become violent during an epilepsy seizure. They also act aggressively when they see other dogs that are injured in a fight. They jump in and try to kill the injured dog.

However, the dogs who respond kindly to the human seizures don't do this. They stay away or try to help the injured dog. Is it possible that "packing" instincts operate in some dogs but "prey" instincts operate in others during a human seizure?

There has also been a case reported in England of a Siamese cat who can predict seizures. If cats and dogs both do it, it may be a drive that runs in both species. However, cats and their relatives in the wild do not travel in packs. It is unlikely the packing instinct operates in cats.

Whether or not an instinct is involved, what specifically sets off the chain of events? It is possible that the dogs notice small changes in the human's behavior. They may see things that the average person would miss, such as a slight trembling or watery eyes. According to veterinarian Andrew T. B. Edney, "Many dog owners will have observed that their dog is capable of detecting when they are going away, even though they believe they have not given any obvious signals. Similar mechanisms are probably at work in seizure-alert behavior."

If dogs can notice slight changes in human behavior, can people notice these changes also?

Sue Miller has learned how to predict seizures in a friend just by watching her. Even from a distance, Sue sees slight posture changes in her friend that signal an oncoming seizure. Nevertheless, behavioral changes cannot totally explain how the dogs can predict seizures. One dog has been able to predict the seizures of an epileptic person in another building with the doors closed. The dog could not see the person and would not have been able to see any change in the person's behavior.

Scientists are currently investigating another theory. They want to know if the dogs can sense electrical changes in the epilepsy victim's brain. Do the brain waves change before and after the dogs start noticing? How do they change? If they receive funding, The Epilepsy Institute would like to conduct a study. They will hook up an EEG to an epilepsy patient's brain. With a dog present, they will videotape a seizure.

According to executive director Pamela Conford, "This process will demonstrate when and if a dog can actually 'seizure alert.' Independent experts will then compare the dog's reactions as seen on videotape to whatever electrical activity was recorded on the EEG."

Still another idea is that the epilepsy victim generates a unique odor through the skin. Possibly the dog smells this odor before the seizure actually occurs. We know that an epilepsy seizure occurs in several stages. The "aura" phase is the first stage of a seizure and does not involve any physical movements. If a chemical were produced during the aura phase, the dog may be detecting its presence by a keen sense of smell.

We also know that dogs are in tune with the feelings of their owners. A dog often knows if you are happy, sad, or angry as soon as you enter the house. Emotions cause chemical changes in the body. If it's possible that a dog senses a body chemistry change, they might be able to do the same thing during a seizure.

According to The Epilepsy Institute's former director Reina Berner, "Some believe dogs can literally smell fear and respond to it in persons who are afraid of them because of the hormonal changes that occur as a result of being scared. Perhaps this is a similar phenomenon."

Dogs themselves may get epilepsy. Can one dog predict the seizures in another dog? Lucky and Gracie are two yellow labradors in Wyoming. Four to six hours before Lucky has a seizure, Gracie runs around nervously. She acts sick herself and tries to throw up. Gracie cuddles with Lucky and licks him. Except during these times, she never shows any affection for him. When Lucky's seizure finally ends, Gracie ignores him until the next seizure comes.

Can dogs be trained as seizure-alert animals? If so, they could help many people who have epilepsy. Dog trainer Sue Miller says that most dogs do have some sensitivity. If a dog shows this ability, it can be praised so it continues to be seizure-alert. Then it might be trained to do specific actions. For example, the dog could rub against the person to cushion a fall, or the dog could summon help by barking or whining. The dog might even be trained to lick the victim's face once a seizure was in progress. This would push aside any items such as clothing or jewelry that might block the victim's breathing.

Currently there are no programs that train seizure-alert dogs. But that will change as people learn about their mysterious talent. And perhaps someday the missing link between dogs and epilepsy will be discovered.

Bibliography

Adams, Cecil. *More of the Straight Dope*. New York: Ballantine, 1988.

———. *The Straight Dope*. New York: Ballantine, 1986.

Adler, Shelley R. "Sudden Unexpected Nocturnal Death Syndrome among Hmong Immigrants: Examining the Role of the 'Nightmare.' " *Journal of American Folklore*, Winter 1991, pp. 54–71.

Arnold, Larry E. "Human Fireballs." *Science Digest*, October 1981, pp. 88–91; 115.

The Associated Press. "Court-martial Urged for Navy Trainer." *Atlanta Journal-Atlanta Constitution*, June 25, 1988, Section A, p. 3.

Berkman, Sue. "Human Diseases Pets Can Get." *Good Housekeeping*, May 1991, p. 213.

Birkby, Robert. "A Walk on the Hot Side." *Mother Earth News*, September/October 1990, pp. 112; 104.

Bixler, Tara. "Seattle DVM's Knowledge, Disability Help in Study of Epilepsy." *DVM Magazine*, April 1992, p. 33.

Blackmore, Susan. "Playing with Fire." *New Scientist*, July 14, 1990, pp. 64–65.

Bolgert, M. "Les Stigmates des Mystiques." *Bulletin de l'Académie nationale de médecine*, January 13, 1981, pp. 35–45.

Browne, Malcolm W. "On the Trail of a 'Wildman,' and Creatures Nearly as Elusive." *The New York Times*, June 19, 1990, pp. C1; C12.

Cebelin, Marilyn S., and Charles S. Hirsch. " 'Scared to Death' May Be a Real Situation." *The American Family Physician*, April 1980, p. 155.

Clark, Matt, and Jeff Copeland. "A Five-Year-Old Dying of Old Age." *Newsweek*, July 23, 1979, p. 72.

Copelan, Rachel. "Stigmata—Passion and Punishment: A Modern Case History." *Journal of the American Society of Psychosomatic Dentistry and Medicine*, Vol. 22, No. 3, 1975, pp. 85–90.

Cory, Christopher T. "Journalists' Oriental Nightmare." *Psychology Today*, August 1981, pp. 19–20.

Danforth, Loring M. *Firewalking and Religious Healing*. Princeton, N.J.: Princeton University Press, 1989.

Diseases. Springhouse, Penn: Springhouse Corporation, 1987.

"A Dog with Sense." *Current Health 1*, December 1990, p. 13.

Doherty, Jim. "Hot Feat: Firewalkers of the World." *Science Digest*, August 1982, pp. 67–71.

Donahue. "Children with Progeria." Multimedia Entertainment, Inc., March 6, 1990.

———. "Children with Progeria." Multimedia Program Production, Inc., February 11, 1982.

Edney, A. T. B. "Dogs as Predictors of Human Epilepsy." *The Veterinary Record*, September 14, 1991, p. 251.

Fisher, Johnnie G., and Edward J. Kollar. "Investigation of a Stigmatic." *Southern Medical Journal*, November 1980, pp. 1461–63; 1466.

Freze, Michael. *They Bore the Wounds of Christ: The Mystery of the Sacred Stigmata*. Huntington, Ind.: Our Sunday Visitor, 1989.

Gardner, Martin. "A Book for Burning." *Nature*, November 26, 1992, p. 396.

Goto, Makoto, Mark Rubenstein, James Weber, Kathryn Woods, and Dennis Drayna. "Genetic Linkage of Werner's Syndrome to Five Markers on Chromosome 8." *Nature*, February 20, 1992, pp. 735–38.

Hansen, James. "Can Science Allow Miracles?" *New Scientist*, April 8, 1982, pp. 73–76.

Hartmann, Ernest. "The Strangest Sleep Disorder." *Psychology Today*, April 1981, pp. 14–18.

Hynes, James V. "Religious Stigmatization" (letter). *The Medical Journal of Australia*, November 3, 1979, p. 490.

———. "Stigmatization" (letter). *The Medical Journal of Australia*, March 6, 1976, pp. 323–24.

Johnson, Richard F. Q. "Warts, Blisters, and Stigmata: Role of Suggestions in Some Unusual Skin Changes." *Journal of the American Society of Psychosomatic Dentistry and Medicine*, Vol. 27, No. 3, 1980, pp. 72–86.

Kelly, Kevin. "Spontaneous Human Combustion." *Whole Earth Review*, Autumn 1986, pp. 52–53.

Kemp, Robert. *Understanding Epilepsy*. London: Tavistock Publications, 1963.

Kong, Dolores, and Bill Lainter. "Some Are Actually Scared to Death Because of Phobias." *Atlanta Constitution*, June 14, 1988, Section D, pp. 1; 4.

Kutner, Lawrence. "Parent & Child: A Child's Scream in the Night May be Quite Normal." *The New York Times*, March 31, 1988, Section C, p. 8.

Lemoine, Jacques, and Christine Mougne. "Why Has Death Stalked the Refugees?" *Natural History*, November 1983, pp. 6–19.

Lin, Jennifer. "A Killer in the Night." *Chicago Tribune*, February 21, 1992, Evening Section, p. 7.

Linedecker, Clifford L. *Unsolved Mysteries*. Boca Raton, Fla.: Globe Communications, 1991.

Magalini, Sergio I. *Dictionary of Medical Syndromes*. Philadelphia: Lippincott, 1971.

Marshall, Eliot. "The Hmong: Dying of Culture Shock?" *Science*, May 29, 1981, p. 1008.

The Maury Povich Show. "Gender Bender: Old Before Their Time." Paramount, Inc., May 11, 1992.

Miller, Peggy Sue. "Pet Therapy Advances: Seizure Alert Dogs." *Dog World*, April 1992, pp. 52–53.

Monagan, David. "Curse of the Sleeping Death." *Science Digest*, April 1982, pp. 36–38.

Munger, Ronald G. and Marshall G. Hurlich. "Hmong Deaths" (letter). *Science*, August 28, 1981, p. 952.

Murphy, Cullen. "A Blaze of Glory." *The Atlantic*, April 1987, pp. 16; 18.

"Mystery Deaths in the Night." *Time*, February 23, 1981, p. 102.

Nadis, Steve. "The Unexpected Talents of Man's Best Friend." *Omni*, May 1992, p. 36.

Petzold, James E. "Southeast Asian Refugees and Sudden Unexplained Death Syndrome." *Social Work*, September 1991, p. 387.

Pflaumer, Sharon. "Seizure-Alert Dogs." *Dog World*, January 1992, pp. 42–44.

Rolbein, Seth. "Bizarre Sleep Disorders." *Good Housekeeping*, May 1989, pp. 69–72.

Rosellini, Lynn. "The Case of the Weeping Madonna." *U.S. News & World Report*, March 29, 1993, pp. 46–55.

Rosenbloom, Arlan L., Samuel Goldstein, and Cecil C. Yip. "Insulin Binding to Cultured Human Fibroblasts Increases with Normal and Precocious Aging." *Science*, July 30, 1976, pp. 412–15.

"Scared to Death." *Science Digest*, November/December 1980, p. 105.

Seligmann, Jean, Joe Contreras, and Peter Rinearson. "The Curse of the Hmong." *Newsweek*, August 10, 1981, p. 47.

Sherman, S. "The Hmong in America." *National Geographic*, October 1988, pp. 586–610.

Schimberg, Albert Paul. *Story of Therese Neumann*. Milwaukee: Bruce Publishing Co., 1947.

Spowart, V. Kaye. "Religious Stigmatization" (letter). *The Medical Journal of Australia*, September 8, 1979, p. 258.

Taylor, John R. "Firewalking: A Lesson in Physics." *The Physics Teacher*, March 1989, pp. 166–68.

Teagarden, Rebecca. "Canines Who Care." *Seattle Post-Intelligencer*, February 1, 1990, pp. C1; C12.

"Terror in the Night." *Science Digest*, March 1981, p. 101.

Tollefsbol, Trygve O., and Robert W. Gracy. "Premature Aging Diseases: Cellular and Molecular Changes." *BioScience*, November 1983, pp. 634–39.

Topping, Audrey. "Hairy Wild Men of China." *Science Digest*, August 1981, pp. 65–67; 113.

United Press International. "CDC Calling Off Surveillance in Mysterious Death Cases." *Boston Globe*, August 17, 1987, p. 5.

Vos Savant, Marilyn. "Ask Marilyn." *Parade Magazine*, June 13, 1993, p. 10.

Wallace, Charles P. "Mysterious Ailment Takes Heavy Toll Among Thais." *Los Angeles Times*, March 23, 1990, Section A, p. 7.

Weatherall, D. J.; J. G. G. Ledingham; and D. A. Warrell, eds. *Oxford Textbook of Medicine*. Oxford: Oxford University Press, 1987.

Westermeyer, Joseph. "Hmong Deaths" (letter). *Science*, August 28, 1981, p. 952.

"When Fear Can Kill." *Family Weekly*, September 20, 1981, p. 22.

Winton, Ronald. "Religious Stigmatization." *The Medical Journal of Australia*, June 16, 1979, pp. 552–53.

Wood, Richard D. "Seven Genes for Three Diseases." *Nature*, March 21, 1991, p. 190.

Wynbrant, James, and Mark D. Ludman. *The Encyclopedia of Genetic Disorders and Birth Defects*. New York: Facts on File, 1991.

Yumin, Gu. "Hairy Child." *China Pictorial*, May 1979, pp. 42–43.

Zhenxin, Yuan, and Huang Wanpo. " 'Wild Man'— Fact or Fiction?" *China Reconstructs*, July 1979, pp. 56–59.

Index

Snipes, Peedie, 77
Spontaneous human com-
  bustion (SHC), 3–13
  age of victims of, 13
  body weight and, 10, 11
  characteristics of victims
    of, 11–13
  early explanations of, 4–5,
    10
  first recorded case of, 4
  limbs undamaged in, 6–7
  nearby items untouched
    in, 7–10
  odor absent from victims
    of, 6
  recent explanations of,
    10–11
  studying, 11, 12
  temperature and, 5–6
Stigmata, *see* Wounds of
  Christ
Stress, sleeping death and,
  61–63, 64
Sudden Unexpected Noctur-
  nal Death Syndrome
  (SUNDS), *see* Sleeping
  death
Sudden Unexplained Death
  Syndrome (SUDS), *see*
  Sleeping death

Temperature:
  heat distinguished from,
    24–28

spontaneous human com-
  bustion and, 5–6

Vantine, Penny, 67–68
Villee, Dr. Dorothy, 72
von Liebig, Baron Justus, 5

Weiss, Sister Maria Fidelis,
  37
Werner's syndrome, 68, 73,
  75
Wildmen, hairy, *see* Hairy
  wildmen
Wounds of Christ, 29–41
  explanations for, 35, 41
  faking of, 33–34, 35–36, 40
  hand stigmata, 37, 38
  invisible stigmata, 36–37
  living stigmatists, 40–41
  pain associated with, 36,
    37
  persons with, 29–33, 34,
    36, 37, 38–41
  as stigmata, 31
  studying persons with,
    40–41

Yang Cher, 56–59
"Yellow rain," 59–60
Ye ren, see Hairy wildmen
Ying Yang, 54
Yu Zhenhuan, 49, 52